莱特兄弟

Heroes and Role Models | Non-Fiction Series

Copyright © 2022 by Level Learning, INC. and Washington Yu Ying PCS™
Original and Edited Text Copyright © 2022 by Washington Yu Ying PCS™

All rights reserved. No part of this book in whole or part may be reproduced without written permission from the publisher.

Published by Level Learning, INC.

Content Contributors:
Washington Yu Ying PCS™
Level Learning - Jingyao Qi

Illustrations by: Josh Taira

Leveling classification based on Level Learning standard. For full description, visit www.levellearning.com

ISBN 978-1-64040-002-3
Simplified Chinese Edition

About Level Learning:
Level Learning provides a literacy focused curriculum specifically designed for K-12 Chinese as a Second Language classrooms. Our program offers 20 levels of specific and detailed objectives, leveled texts and passages, mastery-based online assessment, and analytics to enable data-driven instruction. Level Learning reading curriculum for both literature and informational text emphasize grammar and comprehension skills to help teachers develop confident and independent Chinese language readers. The non-fiction series of books are specifically designed to support our informational text course based on multiple national standards. To learn more about our entire offering, visit www.levellearning.com.

About Washington Yu Ying PCS™:
Washington Yu Ying PCS is a Mandarin English dual language immersion International Baccalaureate (IB) World school. Yu Ying's mission is to inspire and prepare young people to create a better world by challenging them to reach their full potential in a nurturing Chinese/English educational environment. Yu Ying's comprehensive IB, dual immersion curriculum equips students with global competencies for success in the real world. As a leader in immersion education, Yu Ying is determined to advance Chinese language programs and global citizenry education by helping other schools create and strengthen their Chinese programs. For more information, email: products@washingtonyuying.org

莱特兄弟出生在美国，分别出生于1867年和1871年。

他们的爸爸经常出去旅行,旅行回来后会带一些东西给他们。

有一次，爸爸送给莱特兄弟一个玩具。这个玩具是用软木、橡皮筋和纸做的，可以飞起来。

他们非常喜欢这个玩具。从那时开始,他们就想自己发明一个可以让人飞起来的东西。

长大后,他们开了一家自行车店。下班后,他们就一起研制可以飞的东西。

他们看小鸟用翅膀飞行，翅膀后面的羽毛可以让小鸟飞向不同的方向。

莱特兄弟向小鸟学习。他们一次又一次地试验。后来，他们终于发明了第一架可以坐人的飞机。

1903年12月17日,莱特兄弟用他们自己的飞机飞行了59秒,852英尺。

莱特兄弟发明的飞机改变了人类历史,他们是伟大的发明家。

Glossary

	Pinyin	English Definition
兄弟	xiōng dì	brothers
美国	měi guó	United States of America
分别	fēn bié	respectively
经常	jīng cháng	often, frequently
旅行	lǚ xíng	to travel
玩具	wán jù	toy
软木	ruǎn mù	cork, a type of wood
橡皮筋	xiàng pí jīn	rubber band
纸	zhǐ	paper
发明	fā míng	to invent
自行车店	zì xíng chē diàn	bicycle shop
研制	yán zhì	to develop
翅膀	chì bǎng	wing
飞行	fēi xíng	flight, flying

	Pinyin	English Definition
羽毛	yǔ máo	feather
方向	fāng xiàng	direction
学习	xué xí	to learn
试验	shì yàn	to experiment
飞机	fēi jī	airplane
秒	miǎo	second
英尺	yīng chǐ	foot, a measure of distance
人类	rén lèi	human race
伟大	wěi dà	great
发明家	fā míng jiā	inventor

www.ingramcontent.com/pod-product-compliance
Lightning Source LLC
Chambersburg PA
CBHW041223070526
44584CB00001B/73